Creamy Chocolate Cravings

A Chocolate Cookbook

Kristina C. Groves

Recipe For Chocolate Chocolate Chip Cookies

Ingredients

2 cups all-purpose flour
1/2 cup cocoa powder
1 teaspoon baking soda
1 cup softened butter
3/4 cup white sugar
3/4 cup packed brown sugar

2 eggs
1 teaspoon vanilla extract
2 cups semisweet chocolate chips

Directions

Preheat oven to 350 degrees F (175 degrees C). Whisk together the flour, cocoa powder, and baking soda.

Beat the butter, white sugar, and brown sugar with an electric mixer in a large bowl until smooth. Beat in one egg until completely incorporated. Beat in the last egg along with the vanilla. Mix in the flour mixture until just incorporated. Fold in the chocolate chips; mixing just enough to evenly combine. Drop by heaped teaspoonfuls onto ungreased baking sheets.

Bake in the preheated oven until the edges are golden, 9 to 12 minutes. Allow the cookies to cool on the baking sheet for 1 minute before removing to a wire rack to cool completely.

Protein Peanut Butter Chocolate Chip Cookies

Ingredients

1/2 cup butter, softened
1/2 cup peanut butter
1 cup packed brown sugar
1/2 cup white sugar
3 eggs
1 teaspoon vanilla extract
1/3 cup water
1 1/2 cups all-purpose flour
1 cup powdered protein supplement
1 teaspoon baking soda
1/2 teaspoon salt
1 1/3 cups semisweet chocolate chips

Directions

Preheat oven to 350 degrees F (175 degrees C).

In a large bowl, cream together the butter, peanut butter, brown sugar and white sugar until smooth. Beat in the eggs one at a time, then stir in the vanilla and water. Combine the flour, protein powder, baking soda and salt; stir into the creamed mixture. Fold in chocolate chips. Drop dough by heaping spoonfuls onto un-greased cookie sheets.

Bake for 10 to 12 minutes in the preheated oven. Allow cookies to cool on baking sheet for 5 minutes before removing to a wire rack to cool completely.

How To Make Tofu Chocolate Cake

Ingredients

3/4 cup all-purpose flour
1 1/4 cups ground almonds
3/4 cup packed brown sugar, divided
1/2 cup butter
1 1/2 pounds tofu
2/3 cup vegetable oil
1/2 cup orange juice
1/2 cup chocolate liqueur
1/2 cup unsweetened cocoa powder
1 teaspoon almond extract

Directions

Preheat the oven to 325 degrees F (165 degrees C). Lightly grease a 9 inch springform pan.

In a medium bowl, mix together the flour, ground almonds and 1 tablespoon of the brown sugar. Knead in the butter to form a dough. Press the dough firmly into the bottom of the prepared pan.

Using a blender, combine the tofu, remaining sugar, oil, orange juice, chocolate liqueur, cocoa, and almond extract. Blend until smooth and creamy. Spread the batter in an even layer over the prepared crust.

Bake for 1 hour and 15 minutes in the preheated oven. Allow cake to cool to room temperature, then refrigerate overnight. This cake must be thoroughly cold to set properly, otherwise it will be runny like a pudding.

Recipe For Chocolatey Photo Frame

Ingredients

3 tablespoons butter or margarine
1 (10 ounce) package regular marshmallows
6 cups KELLOGG'S(r) COCOA KRISPIES(r) cereal
Canned frosting or decorator gel
Food coloring
Assorted candies and/or multi-colored sprinkles

Directions

In large saucepan melt butter over low heat. Add marshmallows and stir until completely melted. Remove from heat.

Add KELLOGG'S(r) COCOA KRISPIES(r) cereal. Stir until well coated.

Using buttered spatula or wax paper evenly press mixture into 13 x 9 x 2-inch pan coated with cooking spray. Cool.

Trim desired photograph to about 10 x 6-inches. Cut a piece of wax paper to same size as photograph. Place wax paper on center of cereal mixture. Top wax paper with photograph. Decorate edges of cereal mixture with frosting and/or candies. Best if served the same day.

Recipe For Chocolate Peanut Butter Pie

Ingredients

1 cup peanut butter
3/4 cup butter
3 cups confectioners' sugar

2 (8 inch) prepared graham cracker crusts
2 cups milk
1 (3.9 ounce) package instant chocolate pudding mix
1 (8 ounce) container frozen whipped topping, thawed

Directions

In a medium, microwave-safe bowl, combine butter and peanut butter. Heat in the microwave until soft; mix well. Gradually stir in confectioners' sugar until the mixture resembles a soft dough. Spread mixture into 2 pie crusts.

In a small bowl, mix the milk with the instant pudding. Pour over the peanut butter mixture in each crust. Chill until firm.

Top pies with whipped topping when ready to serve.

Chocolate Holiday Cake Recipe

Ingredients

CAKE:
1/2 cup butter
1/2 cup vegetable oil
3 (1 ounce) squares unsweetened chocolate
1 cup water
2 cups all-purpose flour
1 teaspoon baking soda
2 cups sugar
2 eggs, beaten
1/2 cup sour milk*
1 teaspoon vanilla extract
FILLING:
1 (5 ounce) can evaporated milk
3/4 cup sugar
1/4 cup water
1/4 cup chopped seedless raisins
1/2 cup chopped dates
1 teaspoon vanilla extract

1/2 cup chopped pecans
CHOCOLATE ICING:
1 (6 ounce) package semisweet chocolate chips
1/2 cup sour cream
Dash salt
Whipped cream

Directions

In a small saucepan, combine butter, oil and chocolate. Cook over low heat, stirring until chocolate melts. Add water; cool 15 minutes. In another bowl, combine remaining cake ingredients and beat well (*To sour milk, add 1-1/2 teaspoons vinegar to milk; let stand 5 minutes.) Fold chocolate mixture into batter. Pour into two greased and floured 8-in. cake pans. Bake at 350 degrees F for 30-35 minutes or until cakes test done. Cool in pans 5 minutes. Meanwhile, for filling, combine milk, sugar and water in a small saucepan. Cook over medium heat, stirring to dissolve sugar. Add raisins and dates. Cook until thickened, stirring constantly, about 5 minutes. Remove from heat; add vanilla and nuts. Cool. For frosting, melt chips in top of a double boiler over hot water. Remove from heat. Stir in sour cream and salt; beat with a spoon until smooth. Cool 5 minutes or until frosting is of spreading consistency. Place one cake layer, upside down, on a plate. Spread filling on top and place other layer over. Frost entire cake. Chill 1 hour before serving. Serve with a dollop of whipped cream if desired.

Chocolate Chip Pie IV

Ingredients

1 recipe pastry for a 9 inch single crust pie
1 cup white sugar
1/2 cup all-purpose flour
2 eggs
1/2 cup butter, melted and cooled
1 cup pecans, coarsely chopped
1 cup semisweet chocolate chips
1 teaspoon vanilla extract

Directions

In a mixing bowl, mix sugar and flour.

Stir in beaten eggs, butter, nuts, chocolate chips and vanilla. Mix well.

Pour mixture into pie crust. Place pie pan on cookie sheet. Bake in a preheated 325 degree F (165 degree C) oven for one hour.

How To Make Chocolate Hazelnut Cake

Ingredients

1 (18.25 ounce) package devil's food cake mix
1 (3.9 ounce) package instant chocolate pudding mix
1 teaspoon vanilla extract
1/4 cup water
3 cups heavy whipping cream
1 1/2 cups semisweet chocolate chips
1 cup finely chopped toasted hazelnuts
12 hazelnuts

Directions

Prepare cake mix according to package directions, using required ingredients, plus pudding mix, vanilla, and an additional 1/4 cup of water. Spread batter evenly among three greased and floured 9 inch cake pans. Bake at temperature specified on cake mix box for 18 to 22 minutes, or until a toothpick inserted in the center comes out clean. Let cakes cool completely, then chill in refrigerator for 30 minutes.

In a double boiler over simmering water, melt chocolate chips. Gradually add 1/4 cup of the whipping cream, stirring constantly until smooth. Remove from heat and let cool to room temperature. Beat 3/4 cup of whipping cream until soft peaks form. Fold the whipped cream into the cooled chocolate mixture. Stir in 1/2 cup of the finely chopped hazelnuts. Chill 30 minutes.

Beat remaining 2 cups of whipping cream until soft peaks form, then fold in the remaining 1/2 cup of chopped hazelnuts. Chill until ready to frost cake.

Place 1 cake layer on cake plate. Spread 1/2 of the chilled chocolate mixture over top. Add another cake layer. Spread with other 1/2 of chocolate mixture. Top with last cake layer. Frost entire cake with hazelnut-whipped cream. Place 12 whole hazelnuts around top outer edge of cake as a garnish. This cake should be kept in the refrigerator.

Black Forest Chocolate Cake

Ingredients

1 (14 ounce) can fat free sweetened condensed milk
3/4 cup oil substitute
2/3 cup packed brown sugar
2 eggs
1 egg white
1 3/4 cups all-purpose flour
3/4 cup unsweetened cocoa powder
2 teaspoons baking soda
2 teaspoons baking powder
1/2 teaspoon salt
1/2 cup boiling water
1 cup semisweet chocolate chips
1 (21 ounce) can cherry pie filling

Directions

Preheat oven to 350 degrees F (175 degrees C). Coat one 12-cup, fluted tube pan with cooking spray.

Combine flour, cocoa, soda, baking powder, and salt.

In a large bowl, combine condensed milk, oil substitute, brown sugar, eggs, and egg white; mix well. Stir flour mixture into milk mixture just until moistened. Gradually add water. Stir in chips. Pour batter into prepared pan.

Bake for 35 to 40 minutes, or until inserted toothpick comes out clean. Cool cake in pan for 10 minutes. Remove from pan, and top with cherry filling.

Emily's Famous Chocolate Shortbread Cookies Recipe

Ingredients

2 cups confectioners' sugar
1/2 cup Dutch process cocoa powder
3 1/2 cups all-purpose flour
1/2 teaspoon salt
1 1/2 cups unsalted butter, chilled and cubed
1 teaspoon vanilla extract
2 eggs
1 cup chopped semisweet chocolate

Directions

Preheat oven to 350 degrees F (175 degrees C).

In a large bowl, stir together the confectioners' sugar, cocoa, flour and salt until well blended. Cut in the butter until lumps are no larger than peas. Add eggs and vanilla; mix until a stiff dough forms. It may take a minute to come together.

On a lightly floured surface, roll out dough to 1/4 inch thickness and cut into desired shapes using cookie cutters. If the dough is too sticky, chill for a little bit. Place cookies 2 inches apart onto an ungreased baking sheet.

Bake for 8 to 10 minutes in the preheated oven, or until the surface appears dry. Allow cookies to cool for a couple minutes on the baking sheet before removing to wire racks to cool completely. When cookies are completely cool, melt the chocolate over a double boiler or in the microwave. Stir frequently until smooth. Dip cookies or drizzle with the chocolate and place on waxed paper to set.

Chocolate Macaroons II Recipe

Ingredients

3 ounces cream cheese, softened

1/3 cup white sugar

1 teaspoon vanilla extract

1 cup flaked coconut

1/2 cup finely chopped walnuts

1/3 cup butter

1 1/2 cups all-purpose flour

1 cup white sugar

1/4 cup Dutch process cocoa powder

1 egg

3 tablespoons milk

1/2 teaspoon baking soda

Directions

To Make Filling: Beat cream cheese, 1/3 cup sugar and vanilla until soft and smooth. Add coconut and nuts. Chill.

To Make Dough: Beat butter until softened. Add half of flour. Then add 1 cup sugar, cocoa, egg, milk, and baking soda. Beat until combined. Work in the rest of the flour. Chill dough until firm enough to roll.

Place dough between 2 sheets of waxed paper. With rolling pin roll dough in a rectangle 14 x 6 inches. Remove top sheet of waxed paper.

Remove filling from refrigerator and shape into a roll 14 inches long. Place filling on top of dough. Start on one end and roll dough around filling (like rolling up a rug) . Moisten and pinch edges together. Cut roll in half. Wrap in waxed paper and refrigerate for two days.

Cut into 1/4 inch slices (using a very sharp knife or waxed dental floss). Put on greased cookie sheets and bake at 375 degrees F (190 degrees C) for 8 to 10 minutes. Cool on sheet for about 1 minute and then finish cooling on racks.

How To Make Chocolate Jubilees

Ingredients

1 cup butter or margarine, softened
1 cup shortening
2 cups packed brown sugar
1 cup sugar
4 eggs
2 teaspoons almond extract
4 cups all-purpose flour
1 cup quick-cooking oats
1 cup baking cocoa
2 teaspoons baking soda
2 teaspoons salt
1 (16 ounce) jar maraschino cherries, drained and chopped
3 cups semisweet chocolate chips
1 cup sliced almonds

Directions

In a mixing bowl, cream butter , shortening and sugars. Add eggs, one at a time, beating well after each addition. Beat in extract. Combine flour, oats, cocoa, baking soda and salt; gradually add to the creamed mixture. Transfer to a larger bowl if necessary. Stir in cherries, chocolate chips and almonds if desired.

Roll into 1-1/2-in. balls. Place 3 in. apart on ungreased baking sheets. Bake at 375 degrees F for 12-14 minutes or until the edges are firm. Remove to wire racks to cool.

Mellow Chocolate Chip Cookies Recipe

Ingredients

1/2 cup butter, softened
1/2 cup packed brown sugar
1/2 cup white sugar
2 eggs
1/2 teaspoon vanilla extract
1 3/4 cups all-purpose flour
1/4 cup unsweetened cocoa powder
1 teaspoon baking soda

1/4 teaspoon salt

1 cup semisweet chocolate chips

1 cup miniature marshmallows

Directions

Preheat the oven to 375 degrees F (190 degrees C). Grease cookie sheets.

In a large bowl, cream together butter, brown sugar and white sugar until smooth. Beat in the eggs one at a time, then stir in the vanilla. Combine the flour, cocoa, baking soda and salt; stir into the creamed mixture. Mix in the chocolate chips and marshmallows. Drop by rounded spoonfuls onto the prepared cookie sheets about 2 inches apart.

Bake for 8 to 10 minutes in the preheated oven. Allow cookies to cool on baking sheet for 5 minutes before removing to a wire rack to cool completely.

Recipe For Sue's Two-Chocolate Chip Cookies

Ingredients

1 cup butter flavored shortening

3/4 cup white sugar

3/4 cup packed brown sugar

1 teaspoon vanilla extract

2 eggs

2 1/4 cups all-purpose flour

1 teaspoon baking soda

1/4 teaspoon salt

1 cup semisweet chocolate chips

1 cup white chocolate chips

Directions

Preheat oven to 350 degrees F (175 degrees C).

In a medium bowl, cream the shortening, white sugar, and brown sugar together with a wooden spoon. Add eggs and vanilla, mix well. Sift together the flour, baking soda and salt, stir into the creamed mixture. Finally stir in the semi sweet chips and the white chips, if the batter is too stiff, you may need to use your hands.

Drop cookies by heaping spoonfuls onto unprepared cookie sheets. Bake for 7 to 10 minutes in the preheated oven. I always like to take my cookies out of the oven when they are light brown and not yet set. It creates a softer cookie. Allow cookies to cool for a few minutes on the baking sheet before removing to cool on wire racks.

Microwavable Chocolate Fudge

Ingredients

2 cups semisweet chocolate chips
1 (14 ounce) can sweetened condensed milk
2 teaspoons vanilla extract
1 1/2 cups chopped walnuts (optional)
1 cup miniature marshmallows

Directions

Grease an 8×8 inch square pan.

Place the chocolate chips and sweetened condensed milk into a medium sized microwavable bowl. Microwave on high for 2 to 3 minutes, stirring occasionally, until smooth. Stir in the vanilla, then fold in the walnuts and marshmallows. Spread evenly into the prepared pan. Chill until set.

Chocolate Pecan Pie IV Recipe

Ingredients

1 recipe pastry for a 9 inch single crust pie
1/3 cup butter
2 (1 ounce) squares unsweetened chocolate

3 eggs
2/3 cup white sugar
1/2 teaspoon salt
1 cup light corn syrup
1 cup pecan halves

Directions

Preheat oven to 375 degrees F (190 degrees C).

Heat butter and chocolate over low heat, stirring constantly, until chocolate is melted; cool slightly.

With hand beater, beat eggs, sugar, salt, chocolate mixture and corn syrup. Stir in pecans and pour mixture into pie shell.

Bake until set, 40 to 50 minutes. Cool slightly. Serve warm, or refrigerate and serve with nondairy whipped topping.

Costa Rican Coffee Panna Cotta with Bittersweet Chocolate-Rum Sauce

Ingredients

2 teaspoons unflavored gelatin
1/4 cup dark rum
1 1/4 cups whipping cream
1/2 cup dark brown sugar
1 tablespoon instant espresso powder
1 cup coconut milk
1 teaspoon vanilla extract
1 cup sour cream
3/4 cup whipping cream
2 tablespoons dark colored corn syrup
8 ounces bittersweet chocolate, chopped
1 tablespoon dark rum
8 sprigs fresh mint for garnish

Directions

Sprinkle the unflavored gelatin over 1/4 cup of dark rum and allow to soften for 5 minutes.

Meanwhile, stir together 1 1/4 cups of whipping cream, brown sugar, and espresso powder in a saucepan over medium-high heat. Bring to a simmer, stirring until brown sugar has dissolved. Remove from heat, then whisk in gelatin mixture until dissolved.

Whisk in the coconut milk, vanilla extract, and sour cream until smooth. Evenly divide the mixture between eight 3/4 cup custard cups or molds, cover each with plastic wrap, and chill at least 4 hours to overnight.

Bring 3/4 cup whipping cream and corn syrup to a simmer over medium-high heat. Once simmering, remove from heat, and stir in the chocolate until melted and smooth, about 2 minutes. Stir in 1 tablespoon of rum and set aside.

To serve, run a knife around the edge of each mold, then set each cup into a shallow bowl of hot water for 10 seconds to loosen. Invert the mold over a serving plate and remove the panna cotta. Spoon chocolate sauce around each panna cotta and garnish with a sprig of mint.

Passover Chocolate Chip Meringues Recipe

Ingredients

2 egg whites
3/4 cup white sugar
1 teaspoon vanilla extract
1/2 teaspoon salt
1 cup mini semi-sweet chocolate chips

Directions

Preheat oven to 350 degrees F (175 degrees C). Line 2 cookie sheets with aluminum foil.

With an electric beater, beat egg whites until peaks form. Add sugar into the egg whites 1 teaspoon at a time. Gently stir in vanilla and salt, beat until the egg white are stiff and shiny. Fold in chocolate chips.

Drop mixture by teaspoon onto the sheets. Turn off the oven, place the cookies inside the oven and leave them for a few hours or overnight. When you remember to look for them, they'll be ready to eat!

Chocolate Peanut Butter Treats Recipe

Ingredients

1/2 cup light corn syrup
1/2 cup sugar
3/4 cup peanut butter
1/2 teaspoon vanilla extract
2 1/2 cups crisp rice cereal
1/2 cup miniature marshmallows
1/2 cup peanut butter chips
1/2 cup semisweet chocolate chips

Directions

In a small saucepan, combine the corn syrup and sugar. Bring to a boil. Cook and stir for 1 minute. Remove from the heat; stir in peanut butter until melted and blended. Stir in vanilla. Fold in the cereal, marshmallows and chips; stir until blended. Transfer to a greased 8-in. square dish. Cool; cut into squares.

How To Make Chocolate Mint Shot

Ingredients

3/4 fluid ounce Irish cream liqueur
1/2 fluid ounce white chocolate liqueur
1/4 fluid ounce creme de menthe liqueur

Directions

Fill a shot glass half-full with Irish cream. Pour in chocolate liqueur to three-fourths full. Top with creme de menthe.

Raspberry Chocolate Cookies

Ingredients

1/2 cup butter at room temperature
1 cup white sugar
2 eggs
2 teaspoons raspberry extract
1/2 teaspoon almond extract
1/4 cup milk
2 cups all-purpose flour
2 teaspoons baking powder
1/2 cup semi-sweet chocolate chips

Directions

Preheat oven to 350 degrees F (175 degrees C). Grease baking sheets.

Mash the butter and sugar together in a bowl with a wooden spoon until the mixture is creamy and well blended, and beat in eggs, one at a time. Stir in the raspberry extract, almond extract, and milk. In a separate bowl, stir the flour and baking powder together until thoroughly combined, and gradually beat into the butter-egg mixture. Stir in the chocolate chips, and drop by spoonfuls onto the prepared baking sheets.

Bake in the preheated oven until very lightly browned at the edges, 8 to 10 minutes.

Chocolate Peanut Butter Cream Cheese Bars

Ingredients

1 cup all-purpose flour
1/4 cup packed brown sugar
1/2 cup butter, softened
3/4 cup semisweet chocolate chips
2 cups peanut butter chips
1/2 cup white sugar
1/2 cup packed brown sugar
1/3 cup butter, softened
1 (8 ounce) package cream cheese
1 cup unbleached all-purpose flour
1/2 teaspoon baking powder
1/4 teaspoon salt
1 tablespoon rum
1 tablespoon vanilla extract
1/4 cup semisweet chocolate chips
1 tablespoon rum
1 teaspoon water

Directions

Preheat oven to 325 degrees F (165 degrees C).

To Make Crust: Combine 1 cup flour, 1/4 cup packed brown sugar, 1/2 cup butter or margarine and 3/4 cup melted chocolate chips in large bowl. Mix well. Press into bottom of ungreased 11 x 7 inch pan. Top with 2 cups peanut butter chips

To Make Filling: Beat 1/2 cup white sugar, 1/2 cup brown sugar, 1/3 cup butter and 8 oz. cream cheese in large bowl until smooth. Add 1 cup unbleached flour, 1/2 teaspoon baking powder, 1/4 teaspoon salt, 1 tablespoon vanilla and 1 tablespoon rum. Blend well. Spread over peanut butter chips.

Bake until edges are light brown and set, 35-40 minutes. Let cool for 30 minutes.

To Make Glaze: Melt 1/4 cup chocolate chips with 1 tablespoon rum and 1 teaspoon water in small saucepan over low heat. Stir constantly until smooth. Drizzle over filling while warm. Refrigerate 1 hour and cut into bars. Store in refrigerator.

Chocolate Upside-Down Cake

Ingredients

1 1/4 cups water
1/4 cup butter or margarine
1 cup packed brown sugar
1 cup flaked coconut
2 cups semisweet chocolate chips
1 cup chopped pecans
2 cups miniature marshmallows
1 (18.25 ounce) package German chocolate cake mix

Directions

In a small saucepan, heat water and butter until butter is melted. Stir in brown sugar; mix well. Pour into a greased 13-in. x 9-in. x 2-in. baking pan. Sprinkle with coconut, chocolate chips, pecans and marshmallows.

Prepare cake batter according to package directions; carefully pour over marshmallows. Bake at 325 degrees F for 55-60 minutes or until a toothpick inserted near the center comes out clean. Cool for 10 minutes before inverting cake onto a serving plate.

How To Make Frosting for German Chocolate Cake

Ingredients

1 cup half-and-half
1/2 cup butter
1 cup white sugar
3 egg yolks
1 tablespoon cornstarch
1 cup flaked coconut
1/2 cup chopped walnuts

Directions

In a medium saucepan, combine the half and half, butter, sugar, yolks and cornstarch. Bring to a boil over medium heat. Remove from the heat and stir in the coconut and walnuts. Cool to room temperature before frosting cake.

Recipe For Chocolate Pinwheel Bread

Ingredients

1 (.25 ounce) package active dry yeast
1 cup warm milk (110 to 115 degrees F)
1/4 cup sugar
1 teaspoon salt
2 eggs
4 ounces cream cheese, softened
4 cups bread flour
FILLING:
4 ounces cream cheese, softened
1/2 cup confectioners' sugar
2 tablespoons baking cocoa
1 cup semisweet chocolate chips
1 egg, beaten

Directions

In a large mixing bowl, dissolve yeast in warm milk. Add the sugar, salt, eggs, cream cheese and 2 cups flour; beat until smooth. Stir in enough remaining flour to form a soft dough.

Turn onto a floured surface; knead until smooth and elastic, about 6-8 minutes. Place in a greased bowl, turning once to grease top. Cover and let rise in a warm place until doubled, about 1 hour.

Punch dough down. Turn onto a floured surface; divided in half. Roll each portion into a 12-in. x 8-in. rectangle. In a small mixing bowl, beat cream cheese, confectioners' sugar and cocoa until smooth. Spread over each rectangle to within 1/2 in. of edges. Sprinkle with chocolate chips. Roll up jelly-roll style, starting with a short side; pinch seam to seal. Place seam side down in two greased 9-in. x 5-in. x 3-in. loaf pans. Cover and let rise until doubled, about 45 minutes.

Brush tops of loaves with egg. Bake at 350 degrees F for 25 minutes. Cover loosely with foil. Bake 15-20 minutes longer or until loaves sound hollow when tapped. Remove from pans to wire racks to cool.

Recipe For Chocolate Buttercream

Ingredients

12 (1 ounce) squares bittersweet chocolate
2 cups unsalted butter
1 pinch salt
2 eggs
4 cups confectioners' sugar
1 teaspoon vanilla extract

Directions

Melt the bittersweet chocolate, and allow to cool slightly.

Place the butter or margarine, salt, and vanilla in a mixing bowl. Beat with a mixer until very light and airy, about 4 minutes. Add the powdered sugar a little at a time while beating on low speed. Mix well, and beat on medium speed for about 4 minutes. Add the eggs one at a time, and beat for 5 minutes more. Add the melted chocolate, and beat 4 minutes.

Recipe For Oatmeal Chocolate Chip Pancakes

Ingredients

3/4 cup rolled oats
3/4 cup pastry flour
2 teaspoons baking powder
1/2 teaspoon baking soda
1/2 teaspoon sea salt
1/4 cup ground flax seeds

1/4 cup vegan carob chips
1 1/2 cups soy milk

Directions

Preheat a lightly oiled griddle over medium heat.

In a medium bowl, mix rolled oats, pastry flour, baking powder, baking soda, sea salt, flax seeds, and chocolate chips. Gradually blend in soy milk.

Pour batter about 1/4 cup at a time onto the prepared griddle. Cook 1 to 2 minutes, until bubbly. Flip, and continue cooking until lightly browned.

No Bake Chocolate Cookies I Recipe

Ingredients

1 cup butter
2 cups white sugar
1/2 cup evaporated milk
5 teaspoons unsweetened cocoa powder
1 cup flaked coconut
3 cups rolled oats

Directions

Mix oatmeal and coconut together in a large bowl.

Put other ingredients in a saucepan over medium heat, stirring constantly. When mixture comes to a boil, let it boil for 2 minutes.(any longer your cookies will be crumbly, any shorter, your cookies will be gooey)

Remove from heat and pour over the oatmeal-coconut mixture. Working quickly now, mix well and drop by spoon onto waxed paper. Let sit until firm and cool. Excellent for freezing.

Surprise Chocolate Fudge

Ingredients

1 (15 ounce) can pinto beans, rinsed and drained
1 cup baking cocoa
3/4 cup butter or stick margarine, melted
1 tablespoon vanilla extract
7 1/2 cups confectioners' sugar
1 cup chopped walnuts

Directions

In a microwave-safe dish, mash beans with a fork until smooth; cover and microwave for 1-1/2 minutes or until heated through. Add cocoa, butter and vanilla. (Mixture will be thick.) Slowly stir in sugar; add nuts. Press mixture into a 9-in. square pan coated with nonstick cooking spray. Cover and refrigerate until firm. Cut into 1-in. pieces.

Chocolate Snowballs Recipe

Ingredients

1 1/4 cups butter
2/3 cup white sugar
1 teaspoon vanilla extract
2 cups all-purpose flour
1/8 teaspoon salt
1/2 cup unsweetened cocoa powder
2 cups chopped pecans
1/2 cup confectioners' sugar for decoration

Directions

In a medium bowl, cream butter and sugar until light and fluffy. Stir in the vanilla. Sift together the flour, salt, and cocoa; stir into the creamed mixture. Mix in the pecans until well blended. Cover, and chill for at least 2 hours.

Preheat oven to 350 degrees F (175 degrees C). Roll chilled dough into 1 inch balls. Place on ungreased cookie sheets about 2 inches apart.

Bake for 20 minutes in preheated oven. Roll in confectioners' sugar when cooled.

Blackberry-Chocolate Chip Pie Recipe

Ingredients

1 (15 ounce) package pastry for a 9 inch double crust pie
3/4 cup white sugar
1/3 cup all-purpose flour
3/4 teaspoon ground cinnamon
4 cups blackberries
3/4 cup semisweet chocolate chips
1/2 tablespoon lemon juice

Directions

Preheat oven to 425 degrees F (220 degrees C). Place one of the pie crusts into the bottom of a 9 inch pie plate.

In a bowl, mix the sugar, flour, and cinnamon. Gently stir in the blackberries and chocolate chips. Sprinkle with lemon juice. Transfer to the pie crust in the pie plate. Place remaining pie crust over the top, and secure to the bottom crust by pressing with a fork, or fluting with your fingers.

Bake 35 minutes in the preheated oven, until top is golden brown. Cool slightly before slicing.

White Chocolate Chip Oatmeal Cookies Recipe

Ingredients

1 cup butter
1 cup light brown sugar
1 cup white sugar
2 eggs

2 teaspoons vanilla extract
3 cups all-purpose flour
1 teaspoon baking powder
1 teaspoon baking soda
1 teaspoon salt
1 1/2 cups rolled oats
2 cups white chocolate chips
1 cup chopped pecans

Directions

Preheat oven to 350 degrees F (175 degrees C). Lightly grease cookie sheets.

In a medium bowl, cream together the butter, brown sugar and white sugar until smooth. Stir in the egg and vanilla. Sift together the flour, baking powder, baking soda and salt, stir into the creamed mixture. Finally, stir in the rolled oats, white chocolate chips and pecans. Drop by tablespoons onto the prepared cookie sheets.

Bake for 10 to 12 minutes in the preheated oven. Remove from baking sheets to cool on wire racks.

Recipe For Bittersweet Chocolate Mousse Brownies

Ingredients

6 tablespoons unsalted butter
1 (1 ounce) square unsweetened chocolate
1/2 cup white sugar
1 egg
1/4 teaspoon vanilla extract
1/3 cup all-purpose flour
1/8 teaspoon baking soda
1/8 teaspoon salt
4 (1 ounce) squares bittersweet chocolate, chopped
3 tablespoons strong brewed coffee
3 eggs

3/4 cup heavy whipping cream
1/3 cup heavy whipping cream
1 tablespoon confectioners' sugar

Directions

Preheat oven to 350 degrees F (175 degrees C). Line an 8 inch pan with aluminum foil. Make sure to extend the foil beyond the two opposite ends of the pan. This will help in lifting brownies out of pan. Lightly butter bottom and sides of foil-lined pan.

Cut butter into pieces and melt in a saucepan over low heat. Remove pan from heat, add 1 ounce of unsweetened chocolate. Let stand 1 minute, then stir until smooth. Let cool for 10 minutes.

Whisk in 1/2 cup white sugar, 1 egg (make sure egg is at room temperature), and then vanilla. Using a wooden spoon, stir in flour, baking soda and salt just until smooth. Spread dough evenly into pan.

Bake 10-12 minutes until toothpick inserted in center comes out with a moist crumb. Do not overbake. Cool completely on wire rack.

To Make Mousse: Melt 4 ounces of bittersweet chocolate with the coffee in top of a double boiler over hot water. Stir often until smooth. Whisk in 3 egg yolks, one at a time. Remove from heat.

In a chilled medium bowl, beat 3/4 cup heavy cream just until soft peaks form. In another medium bowl, beat 3 egg whites just until soft peaks begin to form. Stir 1/4 of these beaten egg whites into the chocolate/coffee mixture, then carefully fold in the rest

Gently fold in the whipped cream. Spread chocolate mousse evenly over the top of the

How To Make Chocolate Peanut Butter Squares

Ingredients

1 cup butter
4 cups confectioners' sugar
2 cups peanut butter
1 1/2 cups graham cracker crumbs
1/2 cup butter
1 cup semisweet chocolate chips

Directions

Melt 1 cup butter or margarine over low heat. Remove from heat and stir in confectioners' sugar, peanut butter and graham cracker crumbs. Spread mixture in a jelly roll pan. Pat down evenly.

To Make Topping: Melt together 1/2 cup butter or margarine with 1 cup chocolate chips. Spread this mixture over peanut butter mixture. Refrigerate 1/2 hour. Cut into squares.

Recipe For Chocolate Peppermint Candies

Ingredients

3/4 cup sweetened condensed milk
1 1/2 teaspoons peppermint extract
4 cups confectioners' sugar
3 cups semisweet chocolate chips
2 teaspoons shortening

Directions

In a bowl, combine milk and extract. Stir in 3-1/2 to 4 cups confectioners' sugar to form a stiff dough. Turn onto a surface sprinkled lightly with confectioners' sugar. Knead in enough remaining sugar to form a dough that is very stiff and no longer sticky. Shape into 1-in. balls. Place on a waxed paper-lined baking sheet. Flatten into 1-1/2-in. circles. Let dry 1 hour. Turn and let dry 1 hour longer. Melt chocolate chips and shortening in a double boiler or microwave-safe bowl; cool slightly. Dip patties in chocolate mixture and place on waxed paper to harden.

How To Make Pumpkin Chocolate Chip Cookies I

Ingredients

1/2 cup shortening
1 1/2 cups white sugar
1 egg
1 cup canned pumpkin
1 teaspoon vanilla extract
2 1/2 cups all-purpose flour
1 teaspoon baking powder
1 teaspoon baking soda
1 teaspoon salt
1 teaspoon ground nutmeg
1 teaspoon ground cinnamon
1/2 cup chopped walnuts (optional)
1 cup semisweet chocolate chips

Directions

Preheat oven to 350 degrees F (175 degrees C). Grease cookie sheets.

In a large bowl, cream together the shortening and sugar until light and fluffy. Beat in the egg, then stir in the pumpkin and vanilla. Combine the flour, baking powder, baking soda, salt, nutmeg, and cinnamon; gradually mix into the creamed mixture. Stir in the walnuts and chocolate chips. Drop dough by teaspoonfuls onto the prepared cookie sheets.

Bake for 15 minutes in the preheated oven, or until light brown. Cool on wire racks.

Chocolate Cappuccino Cheesecake Recipe

Ingredients

1 cup chocolate cookie crumbs
1/4 cup butter, softened
2 tablespoons white sugar
1/4 teaspoon ground cinnamon

3 (8 ounce) packages cream cheese, softened
1 cup white sugar
3 eggs
8 (1 ounce) squares semisweet chocolate
2 tablespoons whipping cream
1 cup sour cream
1/4 teaspoon salt
2 teaspoons instant coffee granules dissolved in 1/4 cup hot water
1/4 cup coffee flavored liqueur
2 teaspoons vanilla extract

1 cup heavy whipping cream
2 tablespoons confectioners' sugar
2 tablespoons coffee-flavored liqueur

1 (1 ounce) square semisweet chocolate

Directions

Preheat oven to 350 degrees F (175 degrees C). Butter one 9 or 10 inch springform pan.

Combine the chocolate wafer crumbs, softened butter, 2 tablespoons white sugar, and the cinnamon. Mix well and press mixture into the buttered springform pan, set aside.

In a medium sized bowl beat the softened cream cheese until smooth. Gradually add 1 cup white sugar mixing until well blended. Add eggs, one at a time. Beat at low speed until very smooth.

Melt the 8 ounces semisweet chocolate with 2 tablespoons whipping cream in a pan or bowl set over boiling water, stir until smooth.

Add chocolate mixture to cream cheese mixture and blend well. Stir in sour cream, salt, coffee, 1/4 cup coffee liqueur, and vanilla; beat until smooth. Pour mixture into prepared pan.

Bake in the center of oven at 350 degrees F (175 degrees C) for 45 minutes. Center will be soft but will firm up when chilled. Do not over bake. Leave cake in oven with the heat turned off and the door ajar for 45 minutes. Remove cake from oven and chill for 12 hours. Just before serving top cake with mounds of flavored whipped cream and garnish with chocolate leav

Recipe For Chocolate-Covered Cherry Cookies

Ingredients

1/2 cup butter (no substitutes), softened
1 cup sugar
1 egg
1 1/2 teaspoons vanilla extract
1 1/2 cups all-purpose flour
1/2 cup baking cocoa
1/2 teaspoon salt, divided
1/4 teaspoon baking powder
1/4 teaspoon baking soda
1 (10 ounce) jar maraschino cherries
1 cup semisweet chocolate chips
1/2 cup sweetened condensed milk

Directions

In a mixing bowl, cream the butter and sugar. Add egg and vanilla; mix well. Combine the flour, cocoa, 1/4 teaspoon salt, baking powder and baking soda; gradually add to the creamed mixture.

Drain cherries, reserving 1-1/2 teaspoons juice. Pat cherries dry. Shape 1 tablespoon of dough around each cherry. Place 2 in. apart on ungreased baking sheets. Bake at 350 degrees F for 8-10 minutes or until set. Cool on wire racks.

For frosting, in a saucepan, heat chocolate chips and milk until chips are melted; stir until smooth. Remove from the heat. Add reserved cherry juice and remaining salt. Frost cookies.

Recipe For Chocolate Mint Dessert

Ingredients

1 cup butter or margarine, divided
1 (10 ounce) package shredded coconut
1/4 cup packed brown sugar
1/4 cup chopped pecans
4 (1 ounce) squares unsweetened chocolate
1 1/2 cups sugar
1 (12 ounce) can evaporated milk
1 teaspoon vanilla extract
2 quarts mint chocolate chip ice cream, softened

Directions

In a skillet, melt 1/2 cup butter. Add coconut; cook and stir until golden brown. Remove from the heat. Stir in brown sugar and pecans; mix well. Set aside 1 cup. Press remaining coconut mixture onto the bottom and up the sides of a greased 13-in. x 9-in. x 2-in. dish. In a saucepan over medium heat, melt the chocolate and remaining butter. Add sugar and milk. Bring to a slow boil; cook for 5 minutes. Remove from the heat; stir in vanilla. Cool; pour over coconut mixture. Spread ice cream over top. Sprinkle with the reserved coconut mixture. Freeze for 6-8 hours or overnight. Remove from the freezer 15 minutes before serving. The dessert may be frozen for up to 2 months.

Walnut Chocolate Burritos Recipe

Ingredients

5 tablespoons semisweet chocolate chips, divided
2 tablespoons chopped walnuts

1/8 teaspoon ground cinnamon
2 (8 inch) flour tortillas
2 teaspoons vegetable oil
1/2 teaspoon shortening

Directions

In a small bowl, combine 1/2 cup chocolate chips, walnuts and cinnamon. Place tortillas on a microwave-safe plate; microwave, uncovered, on high for 10-15 seconds or until pliable. Spoon chocolate chip mixture down the center of tortillas; fold top and bottom of tortilla over filling and roll up.

In a skillet over medium heat, cook burritos in oil for 1-2 minutes or until lightly browned, turning once. In a microwave-safe bowl, melt shortening and remaining chocolate chips; stir until smooth. Drizzle over burritos. Serve immediately.

Recipe For Chocolate Caramel Brownies

Ingredients

14 ounces caramels
1/2 cup evaporated milk
1 (18.25 ounce) package German chocolate cake mix
1/3 cup evaporated milk
3/4 cup butter, melted
1/4 cup chopped pecans
2 cups milk chocolate chips

Directions

Peel caramels and place in a microwave-safe bowl. Stir in 1/2 cup evaporated milk. Heat and stir until all caramels are melted.

Preheat oven to 350 degrees F (175 degrees C) Grease a 9×13 inch pan.

In a large mixing bowl, mix together cake mix, 1/3 cup evaporated milk, melted butter, and chopped pecans. Place 1/2 of the batter in prepared baking pan.

Bake for 8 minutes.

Place the remaining batter into the fridge. Remove brownies from oven and sprinkle chocolate chips on top. Drizzle caramel sauce over chocolate chips. Remove brownie mix from refrigerator. Using a teaspoon, make small balls with the batter and smash flat. Very carefully, place on top of the caramel sauce until the top is completely covered.

Bake for an additional 20 minutes. Remove and let cool.

Chocolate Zucchini Bread Recipe

Ingredients

3 cups all-purpose flour
3 cups sugar
1/2 cup baking cocoa
1 1/2 teaspoons baking powder
1 1/2 teaspoons baking soda
1 teaspoon salt
1/4 teaspoon ground cinnamon
4 eggs
1 1/2 cups vegetable oil
2 tablespoons butter or margarine, melted
1 1/2 teaspoons vanilla extract
1 1/2 teaspoons almond extract
3 cups grated zucchini
1 cup chopped pecans
1/2 cup raisins

Directions

In a large bowl, combine the first seven ingredients. Combine the eggs, oil, butter and extracts; mix well. Stir into dry ingredients just until moistened. Fold in zucchini, pecans and raisins. Pour into three greased and floured 8-in. x 4-in. x 2-in. loaf pans. Bake at 350 degrees F for 55-60 minutes or until a toothpick inserted near the center comes out clean. Cool for 10 minutes; remove from the pans to wire racks.

Best-Ever Chocolate Fudge Layer Cake

Ingredients

1 (8 ounce) package BAKER'S Semi-Sweet Baking Chocolate, divided
1 (18.25 ounce) package chocolate cake mix
1 pkg. (4 serving size) JELL-O Chocolate Flavor Instant Pudding & Pie Filling
4 eggs
1 cup BREAKSTONE'S or KNUDSEN Sour Cream
1/2 cup oil
1/2 cup water
1 (8 ounce) tub COOL WHIP Whipped Topping, thawed
2 tablespoons PLANTERS Sliced Almonds

Directions

Preheat oven to 350 degrees F. Grease two 9-inch round baking pans. Chop 2 of the chocolate squares; set aside. Beat cake mix, dry pudding mix, eggs, sour cream, oil and water in large bowl with electric mixer on low speed just until moistened. Beat on medium speed 2 min. Stir in chopped chocolate. Spoon into prepared pans.

Bake 30 to 35 min. or until wooden toothpick inserted in centers comes out clean. Cool in pans on wire racks 10 min. Loosen cakes from sides of pans. Invert onto racks; gently remove pans. Cool cakes completely.

Place frozen whipped topping and remaining 6 chocolate squares in microwaveable bowl. Microwave on HIGH 1-1/2 min. or until chocolate is completely melted and mixture is smooth, stirring after 1 min. Let stand 15 min. to thicken. Place one cake layer on serving plate; top with one-fourth of the chocolate mixture and second cake layer. Spread top and side with remaining chocolate mixture. Garnish with almonds. Store leftovers in refrigerator.

Low-Fat Chocolate Cake

Ingredients

1 1/4 cups all-purpose flour
1 cup sugar

1/2 cup baking cocoa
1/4 cup cornstarch
1/2 teaspoon baking soda
1/2 teaspoon salt
4 egg whites
1 cup water
1/2 cup corn syrup
2 teaspoons confectioners' sugar

Directions

In a bowl, combine the first six ingredients. In another bowl, whisk egg whites, water and corn syrup. Stir into dry ingredients. Pour into a 9-in. square baking pan coated with nonstick cooking spray. Bake at 350 degrees F for 30-35 minutes or until a toothpick inserted near the center comes out clean. Cool on a wire rack. Dust with confectioners' sugar.

How To Make Sugar Free Chocolate Macaroons

Ingredients

1 tablespoon unsweetened cocoa powder
12 packets artificial sweetener
4 egg whites
1/8 teaspoon cream of tartar
1 teaspoon vanilla extract

Directions

Preheat an oven to 225 degrees F (110 degrees C). Whisk the cocoa powder and artificial sweetener together in a small bowl; set aside. Line a baking sheet with parchment paper.

Beat egg whites and cream of tartar until foamy in a large mixing bowl. Add the vanilla, and beat until stiff peaks form. Lift your beater or whisk straight up: the egg whites should form a sharp peak that holds its shape. Fold in the cocoa powder mixture until evenly blended. Drop tablespoon-sized dollops of meringue onto the lined baking sheet.

Bake in the preheated oven until the macaroons are crisp and dry, about 1 hour. Cool completely on a wire rack.

Oatmeal Peanut Butter and Chocolate Chip Cookies

Ingredients

3/4 cup butter
1/2 cup white sugar
1 cup packed brown sugar
2 eggs
1/3 cup peanut butter
1/4 cup water
1 teaspoon vanilla extract
1 1/2 cups all-purpose flour
1/2 teaspoon baking soda
2 cups rolled oats
1 cup semisweet chocolate chips

Directions

Preheat oven to 350 degrees F (175 degrees C).

In a medium bowl, cream together the butter, brown sugar and white sugar. Beat in the eggs one at a time, then stir in the peanut butter, water and vanilla. Combine the flour and baking soda, stir into the creamed mixture. Finally, stir in the rolled oats and chocolate chips. Drop by teaspoonfuls onto an unprepared cookie sheet.

Bake for 8 to 10 minutes in the preheated oven, until the cookies are lightly toasted on the edges. Remove from the baking sheet to cool on wire racks.

How To Make Chocolate Almond Velvet

Ingredients

2 pints heavy whipping cream
1 (16 ounce) can chocolate syrup
1 (14 ounce) can sweetened condensed milk
2 teaspoons vanilla extract
1/2 cup slivered almonds, toasted

Directions

In a mixing bowl, combine the first four ingredients; beat until stiff peaks form. Fold in almonds. Spread into an ungreased 13-in. x 9-in. x 2-in. dish. Cover and freeze for at least 4 hours or until firm. May be frozen for up to 2 months. Remove from the freezer 5 minutes before serving.

Creamy Chocolate Cupcakes

Ingredients

1 1/2 cups all-purpose flour
1 cup sugar
1/4 cup baking cocoa
1 teaspoon baking soda
1/2 teaspoon salt
2 eggs, lightly beaten
3/4 cup water
1/3 cup vegetable oil
1 tablespoon vinegar
1 teaspoon vanilla extract
FILLING:
1 (8 ounce) package cream cheese, softened
1/3 cup sugar
1 egg, lightly beaten
1/8 teaspoon salt
1 cup semisweet chocolate chips
1 cup chopped walnuts

Directions

In a large mixing bowl, combine the dry ingredients. Add the eggs, water, oil, vinegar and vanilla; mix well. Pour into 18 greased or paper-lined muffin cups.

For filling, beat cream cheese and sugar in another mixing bowl. Add egg and salt; mix well. Fold in chocolate chips. Drop by tablespoonfuls into center of each cupcake. Sprinkle with nuts. Bake at 350 degrees F for 25-30 minutes.

Chocolate Eclair Cake Recipe

Ingredients

2 (3 ounce) packages instant vanilla pudding mix
3 cups milk
1 (8 ounce) container frozen whipped topping, thawed
1 (16 ounce) package chocolate graham crackers
1/4 cup milk
1/3 cup unsweetened cocoa powder
1 cup white sugar
2 tablespoons butter
1 teaspoon vanilla extract

Directions

In a large bowl, combine pudding mix and 3 cups milk; mix well. Fold in whipped topping and beat with mixer for 2 minutes.

In a buttered 9×13 inch baking dish, spread a layer of graham crackers on the bottom of the dish.

Spread 1/2 of the pudding mixture over crackers, then top with graham crackers. Spread remaining pudding over crackers; top second pudding layer with another layer of crackers.

To make topping: In a medium saucepan over medium-high heat, combine 1/4 cup milk, cocoa and sugar and allow to boil for 1 minute; remove from heat and add butter and vanilla. Mix well and cool.

Pour sauce over graham cracker layer and refrigerate until set; serve.

Oooh Baby Chocolate Prune Cake

Ingredients

9 (1 ounce) squares bittersweet chocolate
2/3 cup unsalted butter
3 eggs
3/4 cup white sugar
1/3 cup all-purpose flour
3/4 cup finely ground almonds
1/2 cup prunes, pitted and chopped
1/2 cup brandy
3 tablespoons water

Directions

Soak prunes overnight in brandy. Melt chocolate and butter or margarine with water.

In a large bowl, beat egg yolks and sugar until pale. Stir in chocolate mixture. Gently mix in flour and ground nuts. Stir in prunes.

In another bowl, beat egg whites to stiff peaks. Carefully fold into cake mixture. Pour into a greased 9 inch round cake tin.

Bake at 375 degrees F (175 degrees C) for 30 – 40 minutes. Remove from oven, and cool on a wire rack. Frost with Chocolate Ganache Frosting.

Chocolate-Banana Tofu Pudding Recipe

Ingredients

1 banana, broken into chunks
1 (12 ounce) package soft silken tofu
1/4 cup confectioners' sugar
5 tablespoons unsweetened cocoa powder

3 tablespoons soy milk

1 pinch ground cinnamon

Directions

Place the banana, tofu, sugar, cocoa powder, soy milk, and cinnamon into a blender. Cover, and puree until smooth. Pour into individual serving dishes, and refrigerate for 1 hour before serving.

How To Make Whip-Up German Chocolate Cookies

Ingredients

1 (18.25 ounce) package German chocolate cake mix

1 cup vanilla yogurt

1/4 cup sour cream

1 egg

1 (16 ounce) container coconut pecan frosting

1/2 cup flaked coconut

1/2 cup chopped pecans

Directions

Preheat oven to 350 degrees F (175 degrees C). Grease cookie sheets.

Empty the package of cake mix into a large bowl. Combine the yogurt, sour cream and egg; stir into the cake mix until well blended. Mix in the coconut pecan frosting, coconut and walnuts. Drop by rounded spoonfuls onto the prepared cookie sheets.

Bake for 8 to 10 minutes in the preheated oven. Allow cookies to cool on baking sheet for 5 minutes before removing to a wire rack to cool completely.

How To Make Vacation Chocolate Monkey Shake

Ingredients

1 cup ice cubes
2 (1.5 fluid ounce) jiggers banana liqueur
4 (1.5 fluid ounce) jiggers creme de cacao liqueur
1 cup chocolate ice cream
1/4 cup chocolate syrup
1 teaspoon vanilla extract
1 cup milk
1 large banana, sliced

1/2 cup sweetened whipped cream
2 tablespoons chocolate shavings, for garnish

Directions

Place the ice, banana liqueur, creme de cacao, ice cream, chocolate syrup, vanilla extract, milk, and banana into a blender. Cover, and puree until smooth. Pour into glasses, and garnish with whipped cream and chocolate shavings to serve.

Recipe For Oatmeal Cranberry White Chocolate Chunk Cookies

Ingredients

2/3 cup butter, softened
2/3 cup packed brown sugar
2 eggs
1 1/2 cups rolled oats
1 1/2 cups all-purpose flour
1/2 teaspoon salt
1 teaspoon baking soda
1 1/4 cups dried cranberries
2/3 cup coarsely chopped white chocolate

Directions

Preheat oven to 375 degrees F (190 degrees C).

In a medium bowl, cream together the butter and brown sugar until light and fluffy. Beat in the eggs one at a time. Combine oats, flour, salt, and baking soda; stir into butter mixture one cup at a time, mixing well after each addition. Stir in dried cranberries and white chocolate. Drop by rounded teaspoons onto ungreased cookie sheets.

Bake for 10 to 12 minutes in preheated oven, or until golden brown. Cool on wire racks.

Chocolate Hazelnut Spread Recipe

Ingredients

1 1/2 cups hazelnuts
3/4 cup semisweet chocolate chips
2 tablespoons honey
2 tablespoons vegetable oil, or as needed (optional)

Directions

Preheat oven to 350 degrees F (175 degrees C).

Line a baking sheet with aluminum foil. Spread hazelnuts on the sheet in an even layer. Bake until skins have split and nuts are fragrant, 10 to 15 minutes; rub with a damp towel and blow the skins away. If they cooled off when you removed the skins, go ahead and warm them in the oven again. This will help them to release more oil.

Combine the nuts and chocolate chips in the bowl of a food processor. Add the honey and process into a smooth paste, adding more oil if needed. Spoon into a container and store at room temperature.

Chocolate Custard Cake Recipe

Ingredients

3 (1 ounce) squares unsweetened chocolate
1/2 cup milk

2/3 cup packed brown sugar
2 eggs, separated
1 3/4 cups cake flour
1 teaspoon baking soda
1 teaspoon baking powder
1/2 teaspoon salt
1/2 cup butter
2/3 cup white sugar
3/4 cup milk
1 teaspoon vanilla extract

Directions

In a saucepan, combine chocolate, 1/2 cup milk, brown sugar, and egg yolks. Cook over low heat, stirring constantly, until custard is thick and smooth. Cool.

Stir together flour, soda, baking powder, and salt.

In a large bowl, cream butter or margarine. Blend in white sugar, beating until light and fluffy. Mix together 3/4 cup milk and vanilla. Stir flour mixture into creamed mixture alternately with flavored milk. Make 3 dry and 2 liquid additions, combining lightly after each. Stir in cooled chocolate custard.

Beat egg whites to form stiff but moist peaks. Fold into cake batter, and beat by hand for 1 minute. Turn batter into two greased and floured 8 inch round cake pans.

Bake at 350 degrees F (175 degrees C) for 25 to 30 minutes, or until cake springs back when lightly touched. Cool layers for 5 minutes, and then remove from pans. Cool completely.

Recipe For Chocolate Pudding Fudge Cake

Ingredients

1 (18.25 ounce) package devil's food cake mix
1 (3.9 ounce) package instant chocolate pudding mix
1 cup sour cream
1 cup milk

1/2 cup vegetable oil
1/2 cup water
4 eggs
2 cups semisweet chocolate chips
6 tablespoons butter
1 cup semisweet chocolate chips

Directions

Preheat oven to 350 degrees F (175 degrees C). Grease and flour a 10 inch Bundt pan.

In a large bowl, combine cake mix, pudding mix, sour cream, milk, oil, water and eggs. Beat for 4 minutes, then mix in 2 cups chocolate chips.

Pour batter into prepared pan. Bake in the preheated oven for 40 to 50 minutes, or until a toothpick inserted into the center of the cake comes out clean. Cool 10 minutes in the pan, then turn out onto a wire rack and cool completely.

To make the glaze: Melt the butter and 1 cup chocolate chips in a double boiler or microwave oven. Stir until smooth and drizzle over cake.

Cranberry Oats with Chocolate

Ingredients

1 1/2 cups sweetened dried cranberries
1 cup orange juice
2/3 cup butter, softened
2/3 cup brown sugar
2 eggs
1 1/2 cups rolled oats
1 1/2 cups all-purpose flour
1/2 teaspoon baking soda
1/2 teaspoon baking powder
1/2 teaspoon salt
1 cup chopped white chocolate

Directions

In a small bowl, soak dried cranberries in orange juice to soften, about 30 minutes. Preheat the oven to 325 degrees F (165 degrees C).

In a large bowl, cream together the butter and brown sugar until smooth. Beat in the egg. Combine the oats, flour, baking soda, baking powder and salt; stir into the creamed mixture. Drain cranberries and stir into the dough along with white chocolate making sure not to over-mix and make tough cookies. Drop by rounded spoonfuls onto ungreased cookie sheets.

Bake for 10 to 12 minutes in the preheated oven. Allow cookies to cool on baking sheet for 5 minutes before removing to a wire rack to cool completely..

Chocolate Cheesecake IV

Ingredients

1 (9 inch) graham cracker crust
2 (8 ounce) packages cream cheese
2 cups semisweet chocolate chips
1 (14 ounce) can sweetened condensed milk
2 eggs
1 teaspoon vanilla extract

Directions

Preheat oven to 325 degrees F (165 degrees C). Melt chocolate chips in a double boiler or in the microwave, stirring occasionally until smooth. set aside.

In a medium bowl, mix the cream cheese until smooth and creamy. Gradually add the sweetened condensed milk, then beat in the eggs and vanilla. Finally, stir in the melted chocolate. Pour into the prepared crust.

Bake for 1 hour in the preheated oven, until the center is set. Allow cheesecake to cool to room temperature, then refrigerate at least 4 hours before serving.

Polish Style Chocolate Cake

Ingredients

3/4 cup butter
1/4 cup shortening
2 cups white sugar
2 eggs
1 3/4 cups all-purpose flour
3/4 cup unsweetened cocoa powder
3/4 teaspoon baking soda
3/4 teaspoon baking powder
1 3/4 cups milk
1 teaspoon vanilla extract
1 (8 ounce) container frozen whipped topping, thawed
3 bananas

Directions

Preheat oven to 350 degrees F (175 degrees C). Grease and flour a 9×13 inch pan. Sift together the flour, cocoa, baking soda and baking powder. Set aside.

In a large bowl, cream together the butter, shortening and sugar until light and fluffy. Add the eggs one at a time, beating well with each addition, then add the vanilla. Add the flour mixture alternately with the milk. Mix to combine.

Pour batter into a 9×13 inch pan. Bake for 30 minutes in the preheated oven, or until a toothpick inserted into the cake comes out clean. Allow to cool.

Spread whipped topping over cooled cake and place sliced bananas on top. Store in refrigerator.

White Chocolate Macadamia Creme Brulee Recipe

Ingredients

6 tablespoons chopped and toasted macadamia nuts
1/2 cup white sugar
2 cups whipping cream
4 ounces white chocolate, chopped
4 egg yolks
1 tablespoon vanilla extract
1/2 cup brown sugar, firmly packed

Directions

Preheat oven to 300 degrees F (150 degrees C).

Set 6 (4-ounce) ramekins in a deep baking dish. Put 1 tablespoon of the macadamia nuts into each of the ramekins.

In a saucepan, stir the cream and sugar over medium heat. When the mixture comes to a slow simmer, add the white chocolate and remove from the heat. Whisk until the chocolate has completely melted. Stir in the egg yolks, one at a time, continuing to whisk until combined. Stir in the vanilla extract. Divide the mixture evenly between the ramekins. Place the dish into the oven and then pour water into baking dish until ramekins are 3/4 submerged.

Bake in preheated oven until custard has set, about 45 minutes. Remove pan and turn oven to broil.

Sprinkle the brown sugar over each of the ramekins. Place pan under broiler until sugar has melted and caramelized, about 5 minutes.

Remove ramekins from water bath. Allow to cool for about 15 minutes. I prefer to chill these in the fridge before serving however they are just as heavenly served warm.

Recipe For Chocolate Snaps Sugar Cookie

Ingredients

2 cups all-purpose flour
1 teaspoon baking soda
1/2 teaspoon salt

3 tablespoons margarine
1/2 cup unsweetened cocoa powder
3/4 cup butter, softened
1 cup white sugar
1/2 cup packed brown sugar
2 eggs
1 teaspoon vanilla extract
1/2 cup white sugar

Directions

Sift together the flour, baking soda and salt; set aside. In a medium saucepan over medium heat, melt margarine. Stir in cocoa, remove from heat and set aside to cool. In a large bowl, cream together the butter, 1 cup white sugar and brown sugar until fluffy. Beat in the eggs one at a time, then stir in the cocoa mixture and the vanilla. Blend in the sifted ingredients to form a soft dough. Cover dough and refrigerate for at least an hour or two.

Preheat oven to 350 degrees F (175 degrees C). Roll chilled dough into 1 inch balls, roll them in the remaining sugar and place them 2 to 3 inches apart onto ungreased cookie sheets.

Bake for 8 to 10 minutes in the preheated oven. Allow cookies to cool on baking sheet for 5 minutes before removing to a wire rack to cool completely.

Chocolate Cream Cheese Frosting

Ingredients

4 (1 ounce) squares unsweetened chocolate
1 (8 ounce) package cream cheese
4 cups confectioners' sugar
1 tablespoon vanilla extract
1/8 teaspoon salt
2 tablespoons evaporated milk

Directions

Have all ingredients at room temperature. Melt the chocolate in a double boiler or microwave oven.

In a large bowl, beat cream cheese until fluffy. Pour melted chocolate into cream cheese and mix on medium speed until well blended. Add vanilla and pinch of salt. Slowly mix in the confectioners sugar.

Scrape the sides of the bowl and increase mixer speed to medium-high. Slowly add evaporated milk until the frosting is spreading consistency.

How To Make German Chocolate Upside Down Cake

Ingredients

1 1/4 cups water
1/4 cup butter
1 cup packed brown sugar
1 cup flaked coconut
2 cups miniature marshmallows
1 cup chopped walnuts

4 (1 ounce) squares German sweet chocolate
1/2 cup water
2 1/2 cups all-purpose flour
1 1/2 cups white sugar
1 teaspoon baking soda
1/2 teaspoon salt
1 cup sour cream
1/2 cup butter, softened
1 teaspoon vanilla extract
3 eggs

Directions

Preheat oven to 350 degrees F (175 degrees C). Not necessary to grease pan.

In a sauce pan, combine 1 1/4 cup water and 1/4 cup butter or margarine. Heat until butter melts, then stir in brown sugar and coconut. Pour into ungreased 9×13 inch pan. Sprinkle marshmallows and nuts over top. set aside.

For the cake: in a saucepan over low heat, combine chocolate with 1/2 cup water. Heat, stirring, until chocolate is melted. Remove from heat.

In a large bowl, mix flour, sugar, soda and salt. Add sour cream, 1/2 cup butter or margarine, vanilla and eggs. Add chocolate mixture and beat 3 minutes. Carefully spoon batter over coconut marshmallow mixture in pan.

Bake at 350 degrees F (175 degrees C) for 40 to 50 minutes, or until toothpick inserted into center comes out clean. Place pan on foil or cookie sheet to guard against spillage.

Christmas Chocolate Town Cake Recipe

Ingredients

1/2 cup unsweetened cocoa powder
1/2 cup boiling water
2/3 cup shortening
1 3/4 cups white sugar
1 teaspoon vanilla extract
2 eggs
2 1/2 cups all-purpose flour
1 teaspoon baking soda
1 teaspoon salt
1 1/3 cups buttermilk

Directions

Preheat oven to 350 degrees F (175 degrees C). Grease and flour 2 – 9 inch pans. Sift together the flour, baking soda and salt. Set aside.

Combine cocoa and boiling water in small bowl to form a smooth paste. Cool slightly.

In a large bowl, cream together the shortening, sugar and vanilla until light and fluffy. Beat in the eggs one at a time. Beat in the flour mixture alternately with the buttermilk, mixing just until incorporated. Blend in cocoa paste.

Divide batter into 2 prepared 9 inch pans. Bake in the preheated oven for 35 to 40 minutes, or until a toothpick inserted into the center of the cake comes out clean. Cool 10 minutes in pans then turn out onto wire rack and cool completely.

How To Make Chocolate Surprise

Ingredients

1/2 cup butter, softened
1 cup white sugar
1 egg
1/4 cup milk
1 teaspoon vanilla extract
1 3/4 cups all-purpose flour
1/3 cup unsweetened cocoa powder
1/2 teaspoon baking soda
18 large marshmallows, halved

1 cup white sugar
1/2 cup unsweetened cocoa powder
1/4 cup milk
1 teaspoon vanilla extract
1/4 cup butter
18 pecan halves

Directions

Preheat oven to 350 degrees F (175 degrees C). Grease cookie sheets.

In a large bowl, cream together 1/2 cup butter and 1 cup sugar until smooth. Beat in the egg, then stir in the 1/4 cup milk and vanilla. Combine the flour, 1/3 cup cocoa and baking soda; stir into the creamed mixture. Drop by heaping teaspoonfuls onto the prepared cookie sheet.

Bake for 8 minutes in the preheated oven. Remove cookie sheet and press marshmallow halves into the center of each cookie cut side down. Return the cookies to the oven for an additional 2 minutes. Remove from the oven and press lightly on the cookies to flatten slightly. Remove cookies to wire racks to cool.

To make the icing: In a small saucepan over medium heat, combine 1 cup sugar, 1/2 cup cocoa, 1/4 cup milk, 1 teaspoon vanilla and 1/4 cup butter. Bring the mixture to a boil, stirring occasionally, and let boil for 1 minute. Brush the cookies with the frosting then top each one with a pecan half before the icing sets.

Peppermint Chocolate Bars

Ingredients

1/2 cup butter (no substitutes)
2 (1 ounce) squares unsweetened chocolate
2 eggs
1 cup sugar
2 teaspoons vanilla extract
1/2 cup all-purpose flour
1/2 teaspoon salt
1/2 cup chopped pecans or walnuts
FROSTING:
1/4 cup butter (no substitutes), softened
2 cups confectioners' sugar
1 teaspoon peppermint extract
3 tablespoons whipping cream
TOPPING:
1 (1 ounce) square semisweet chocolate
1 tablespoon butter (no substitutes)

Directions

In a microwave or double boiler, melt butter and chocolate; cool slightly. In a mixing bowl, beat the eggs, sugar and vanilla. Add the chocolate mixture and mix well. Combine flour and salt; gradually add to chocolate mixture. Stir in nuts.

Spread into a greased 13-in. x 9-in. x 2-in. baking pan. Bake at 350 degrees F for 16-20 minutes or until a toothpick inserted near the center comes out clean. Cool on a wire rack.

In a mixing bowl, cream butter, sugar and extract. Add enough cream until frosting reaches spreading consistency. Frost cooled bars. Melt chocolate and butter; drizzle over frosting. Cut into bars.

Chocolate Butterschnapps Cake Recipe

Ingredients

3 (1 ounce) squares unsweetened chocolate
6 tablespoons butter
2 eggs
1 1/3 cups white sugar
3/4 cup all-purpose flour
3/4 teaspoon baking powder
1/2 teaspoon salt
1/2 cup butterscotch schnapps, divided
1 teaspoon vanilla extract
1/2 teaspoon almond extract
1/4 cup semisweet chocolate chips
1/2 cup butterscotch chips
1/4 cup slivered almonds
1 cup heavy whipping cream
2 cups semisweet chocolate chips
2 tablespoons amaretto liqueur

Directions

Melt unsweetened chocolate and butter or margarine in the top of a double boiler or in a bowl in the microwave. Stir until smooth. Set aside to cool.

In a large bowl, beat eggs well. Gradually add sugar, and beat until fluffy. Add cooled chocolate mixture slowly; mix well. Stir in 1/4 cup schnapps, almond extract, and vanilla. Briefly stir together flour, baking powder, and salt; gradually add flour mixture to chocolate mixture. Mix only to combine. Stir in chips with spatula. Divide batter into two greased and floured, 8 inch, round cake pans.

Bake at 350 degrees F (175 degrees C) for 20 to 25 minutes, or until the cake tests done. Cool for 10 minutes in the pans.

Meanwhile, bring the cream to a boil in a medium saucepan. Remove from heat, and stir in 12 ounces chocolate chips. Cover, and let stand 10 minutes. Remove lid, and stir in amaretto.

Remove layers from pans. Brush with remaining schnapps. Place one layer on a serving plate. Pour 1/3 of the glaze over the layer, and then place the second layer over the first. Pour remaining glaze over the whole cake. Decorate with slivered almonds.

How To Make Chocolate-Filled Spritz

Ingredients

1 cup butter (no substitutes), softened
2/3 cup sugar
1 egg
1/2 teaspoon vanilla extract
1/2 teaspoon lemon or orange extract
2 1/4 cups all-purpose flour
1/4 teaspoon baking powder
1/4 teaspoon salt
4 (1 ounce) squares semisweet chocolate

Directions

In a mixing bowl, cream butter and sugar. Beat in the egg and extracts. Combine the dry ingredients; gradually add to the creamed mixture. Using a cookie press fitted with the disk of your choice, press dough 2 in. apart onto ungreased baking sheets. Bake at 350 degrees F for 10-12 minutes or until set (do not brown). Remove to wire racks to cool. Melt the chocolate; spread over the bottom of half of the cookies; top with remaining cookies.

Chocolate Pudding Cake I

Ingredients

1 (10 inch) angel food cake
1 (8 ounce) container frozen whipped topping, thawed
1 (5 ounce) package non-instant chocolate pudding mix
1 (1.55 ounce) bar milk chocolate

Directions

Tear Angel food cake into bite size pieces into a 9×13 inch cake pan (preferably glass).

Prepare chocolate pudding as directed on package. Gently spread over the top of cake pieces, spreading to edges of pan.

Carefully spread whipped topping over chocolate pudding, spreading to edges of pan and taking care not to mix with pudding.

Using a cheese grater or vegetable peeler, grate chocolate bar over the whipped topping.

Chill until ready to serve, at least one hour.

Recipe For Chocolate Sauerkraut Cake I

Ingredients

2/3 cup shortening
1 1/2 cups white sugar
2 1/4 cups all-purpose flour
1 teaspoon baking soda
1 teaspoon baking powder
1/4 teaspoon salt
1/2 cup unsweetened cocoa powder
3 eggs

1 1/4 teaspoons vanilla extract
1 cup water
1/2 cup drained and chopped sauerkraut

Directions

Cream shortening and sugar. Add eggs one at a time, beating well after each addition. Stir in vanilla.

In another bowl, whisk together flour, baking soda, baking powder, salt and cocoa. Add flour mixture to creamed ingredients alternately with the water, ending with dry ingredients. Mix well until smooth. Blend in sauerkraut.

Bake at 350 degrees F (175 degrees C) for 30 to 35 minutes. Top with Fluffy Creamy Frosting.

Alaskan Chocolate Scrambled Eggs

Ingredients

5 eggs, beaten
1 cup milk
3 tablespoons instant white chocolate flavored coffee mix powder
1 tablespoon black pepper

Directions

In a medium bowl, thoroughly mix eggs, milk, instant white chocolate flavored coffee mix powder and black pepper.

Pour egg mixture into a medium skillet over medium heat. Cook, stirring often, 5 to 10 minutes, until eggs are firm.

Recipe For TOLL HOUSE(r) Chocolate Cheesecake

Ingredients

1 (16.5 ounce) package NESTLE(r) TOLL HOUSE(r) Refrigerated Chocolate Chip Cookie Dough
2 (8 ounce) packages cream cheese, softened
1 cup granulated sugar
4 (1 ounce) packets NESTLE(r) TOLL HOUSE(r) CHOCO BAKE(r) Pre-Melted Unsweetened Chocolate Flavor
2 (8 ounce) containers frozen whipped topping, thawed
1/2 cup NESTLE(r) TOLL HOUSE(r) Semi-Sweet Chocolate Morsels, melted

Directions

Preheat oven to 375 degrees F. Grease a 9-inch springform pan.

Slice dough into 16 pieces. Cover bottom of prepared pan with pieces. Allow to soften for 5 to 10 minutes. Using fingertips, pat dough gently to cover bottom.

Bake for 15 to 17 minutes or until light golden brown. Cool completely in pan on wire rack.

Combine cream cheese, sugar and CHOCO BAKE in a large mixing bowl until well blended. Add whipped topping; stir until just blended. Spoon over cookie crust; smooth top. Drizzle with melted chocolate. Cover; refrigerate for 3 to 4 hours or overnight. Remove sides of pan.

Chocolate Chip Eggnog Balls

Ingredients

2 (3 ounce) packages cream cheese, softened
4 cups sifted confectioners' sugar
1 tablespoon heavy cream
1 teaspoon brandy
1/2 teaspoon salt
1/4 teaspoon ground cinnamon
1/8 teaspoon ground nutmeg

1/2 cup miniature semisweet chocolate chips
1 1/4 cups finely chopped pecans

Directions

In a large bowl, cream together the cream cheese and confectioners' sugar. Beat in the heavy cream and brandy. Combine the salt, cinnamon and nutmeg, stir into the cream cheese mixture along with the mini chips to form a smooth dough. Drop by rounded spoonfuls onto a cookie sheet. Chill for 5 minutes.

Roll the chilled dough into balls and roll them in the chopped pecans to coat completely. Serve chilled.

Recipe For Easy Chocolate Drops

Ingredients

1 cup semisweet chocolate chips
1 cup butterscotch chips
1 cup shoestring potato sticks
1 cup salted peanuts

Directions

In a 2-qt. microwave-safe bowl, heat chips on high for 2 minutes or until melted, stirring once. Stir in potato sticks and peanuts. Drop by teaspoonfuls onto waxed paper-lined baking sheets. Chill until set, about 15 minutes. Store in air-tight containers.

How To Make Crispy Chocolate Squares

Ingredients

1 (10.5 ounce) package miniature marshmallows
1 cup peanut butter
1 cup semisweet chocolate chips
1/2 cup butter or margarine

2 cups crisp rice cereal
1 cup salted peanuts
FROSTING:
1 cup semisweet chocolate chips
1/4 cup butter or margarine
1/4 cup milk
2 cups confectioners' sugar
1 teaspoon vanilla extract

Directions

In a large microwave-safe bowl, combine the marshmallows, peanut butter, chocolate chips and butter. Cover and microwave on high for 2-1/2 minutes. Stir until well blended (the mixture will be lumpy). Add cereal and peanuts; stir until well coated. Spread into a greased 13-in.x 9-in. x 2-in. pan. For the frosting, combine chocolate chips, butter and milk in another microwave-safe bowl. Cover and microwave on high for 1-1/2 sugar and vanilla. With an electric mixer, beat frosting until smooth. Spread over the cereal mixture. Cover and refrigerate for 2 hours or until firm. Cut into squares.

How To Make Chocolate Covered Cherry Shooters

Ingredients

2 (1.5 fluid ounce) jiggers amaretto liqueur
1 teaspoon grenadine syrup
2 teaspoons chocolate syrup
2 teaspoons heavy cream

Directions

Fill a cocktail shaker with ice, and pour in the amaretto, grenadine syrup, chocolate syrup, and heavy cream. Shake well, and strain into shot glasses.

How To Make Chocolate Chip Amaretto Pound Cake

Ingredients

3 eggs
1 (18.25 ounce) package devil's food cake mix
1/3 cup vegetable oil
1 cup water
2 tablespoons almond extract
1 cup semisweet chocolate chips
1/4 cup confectioners' sugar for dusting

Directions

Preheat the oven to 350 degrees F (175 degrees C). Grease the bundt pan.

Mix eggs, cake mix, oil, water and almond extract with electric beater. Stir in chocolate chips.

Pour into prepared pan. Bake approximately 1 hour or until cake tests done. Cool, then dust with confectioners' sugar.

Double Chocolate Chip Cookies

Ingredients

1 cup butter or margarine, softened
1 cup sugar
1/2 cup packed dark brown sugar
1 teaspoon vanilla extract
1 egg
1/3 cup baking cocoa
2 tablespoons milk
1 3/4 cups all-purpose flour
1/4 teaspoon baking powder

1 cup chopped walnuts
1 cup semisweet chocolate chips

Directions

In a large mixing bowl, cream the butter, sugars and vanilla. Beat in egg. Add cocoa and milk. Combine flour and baking powder; fold into creamed mixture with walnuts and chocolate chips.

Roll teaspoonfuls of dough into balls; place 2 in. apart on ungreased baking sheets. Bake at 350 degrees F for 10-12 minutes. Cool for 5 minutes before removing to wire racks to cool.

EAGLE BRAND(r) Quick Chocolate Mousse

Ingredients

1 (14 ounce) can EAGLE BRAND(r) Sweetened Condensed Milk
1 cup cold water
1 (4 serving size) package instant chocolate flavor pudding mix
1 cup whipping cream, whipped

Directions

In large bowl, combine sweetened condensed milk and water. Add pudding mix; beat well. Chill 5 minutes. Fold in whipped cream. Spoon into serving dishes; chill. Garnish as desired. Store leftovers covered in refrigerator.

Recipe For Candi's Chocolate Peanut Butter Chip Cookies

Ingredients

2 1/2 cups all-purpose flour
1 teaspoon baking soda
1 teaspoon salt

1/3 cup unsweetened cocoa powder
1/2 cup butter, softened
1 (3 ounce) package cream cheese, softened
1 cup white sugar
1 cup brown sugar
2 eggs
1 teaspoon vanilla extract
1 tablespoon applesauce
2 cups peanut butter chips

Directions

Preheat the oven to 375 degrees F (190 degrees C). Stir together the flour, baking soda, salt and cocoa; set aside.

In a large bowl, cream together the butter, cream cheese, white sugar and brown sugar until smooth. Beat in the eggs one at a time, then stir in the vanilla and applesauce. Blend in the dry ingredients to form a dough. Fold in the peanut butter chips by hand. Drop the dough by teaspoons two inches apart on a ungreased cookie sheet.

Bake for 8 to 10 minutes in the preheated oven. Allow cookies to cool on baking sheet for 5 minutes before removing to a wire rack to cool completely.

Chocolate Chip Oat Bars Recipe

Ingredients

1 cup all-purpose flour
1 cup quick-cooking oats
3/4 cup packed brown sugar
1/2 cup cold butter or margarine
1 (14 ounce) can sweetened condensed milk
1 cup chopped pecans
1 cup semisweet chocolate chips

Directions

In a bowl, combine the flour, oats and brown sugar. Cut in the butter until crumbly. Press half of the mixture into a greased 13-in. x 9-in. x 2-in. baking pan. Bake at 350 degrees F for 8-10 minutes. Remove from the oven. Spread condensed milk evenly over the crust. Sprinkle with pecans and chocolate chips. Top with remaining oat mixture and pat lightly. Bake for 25-30 minutes or until lightly browned. Cool in pan on a wire rack.

Recipe For White Chip Chocolate Cookies

Ingredients

1 cup butter, softened
2 cups white sugar
2 eggs
2 teaspoons vanilla extract
2 cups all-purpose flour
3/4 cup unsweetened cocoa powder
1 teaspoon baking soda
1/2 teaspoon salt
1 2/3 cups white chocolate chips

Directions

Preheat oven to 350 degrees F (175 degrees C).

In a large bowl, cream together the butter and sugar until smooth. Beat in the eggs one at a time, then stir in the vanilla. Combine the flour, cocoa, baking soda and salt; stir into the creamed mixture. Fold in the white chocolate chips. Drop by rounded teaspoonfuls onto ungreased cookie sheets.

Bake for 8 to 10 minutes in the preheated oven, until cookies are set. Allow cookies to cool on baking sheet for 5 minutes before removing to a wire rack to cool completely.

How To Make Chocolate Chip Pie III

Ingredients

1 cup white sugar
2 eggs, lightly beaten
1/2 cup chopped pecans
1/2 cup all-purpose flour
1/2 cup butter, melted
1 cup semisweet chocolate chips
1 (9 inch) pie shell

Directions

Preheat oven to 325 degrees F (165 degrees C).

Combine cooled melted butter or margarine and sugar, eggs, pecans, flour and chocolate chips; mix well. Pour the mixture into the unbaked pastry shell and bake in the preheated oven for about 1 hour. Let cool and serve.

Instant Chocolate Oatmeal Cookies Recipe

Ingredients

3 cups quick cooking oats
1 teaspoon vanilla extract
1 pinch salt
1 cup chopped pecans (optional)
2 cups white sugar
1/2 cup evaporated milk
1/2 cup butter
2 tablespoons unsweetened cocoa powder

Directions

In large bowl combine oats, vanilla and salt. Stir in pecans.

In a medium saucepan, combine sugar, evaporated milk, butter and cocoa. Bring to a boil. Remove from heat, stir in oats mixture.

Drop mixture by teaspoonfuls onto waxed paper. Let cool.

Sweet and Spicy Chocolate Cake

Ingredients

1 1/3 cups all-purpose flour
1/3 cup unsweetened cocoa powder
1/2 teaspoon baking powder
1 cup chopped dried apricots
1 cup boiling water
5 ounces almond paste
3/4 cup white sugar
4 eggs
2/3 cup whole milk
3 ounces bittersweet chocolate, chopped
2/3 cup finely chopped crystallized ginger
3/4 cup unsalted butter, melted

Directions

Preheat oven to 350 degrees F (175 degrees C). Grease and flour a 9×5 inch loaf pan. Sift together flour, cocoa, and baking powder.

Soak chopped apricots in boiling water for 1 to 2 minutes. Drain, and pat dry with paper towels.

In a large mixing bowl, mix almond paste and sugar with an electric mixer until the mixture looks sandy. Beat in eggs one at a time; beat for 2 minutes after each addition. Continue beating for about 10 minutes; mixture should look thick and creamy.

Mix in milk, and then flour mixture. Mix only to combine the dry with the wet ingredients. Do not overbeat. Fold in apricots, chocolate, crystallized ginger, and melted butter. Transfer batter to prepared loaf pan.

Bake in preheated oven for about 1 hour, until done. Cool for 10 minutes in pan. Remove from pan, and place on a wire rack to cool completely.

How To Make White Chocolate Macadamia Cookies

Ingredients

1/2 cup butter or margarine, softened
2/3 cup sugar
1 egg
1 teaspoon vanilla extract
1 1/8 cups all-purpose flour
1/2 teaspoon baking soda
1 (3.5 ounce) jar macadamia nuts, chopped
1 cup vanilla chips

Directions

In a mixing bowl, cream butter and sugar. Beat in the egg and vanilla. Combine flour and baking soda; gradually add to creamed mixture. Stir in nuts and vanilla chips. Drop by heaping teaspoonfuls 2 in. apart onto ungreased baking sheets. Bake at 350 degrees F for 10-12 minutes or until golden brown. Cool for 1 minute before removing to wire racks.

Crisp Chocolate Rolls Recipe

Ingredients

1/2 cup butter, softened
1/2 cup white sugar
1 teaspoon vanilla extract
2 egg whites
2/3 cup all-purpose flour
3 (1 ounce) squares semisweet chocolate
1/4 teaspoon vegetable oil

Directions

In a large mixing bowl, cream 1/2 cup butter or margarine, 1/2 cup sugar, and 1 teaspoon vanilla until light and fluffy. Add egg whites; blend well. Gradually add flour and blend well.

Drop batter by teaspoons 1 inch apart on an ungreased baking sheet. Spread with the back of a spoon into 3-inch rounds.

Preheat oven to 375 degrees F (190 degrees C).

Bake for 5 minutes or until edges are light brown. Working with 1 cookie at a time, loosen from baking sheet with a spatula and then quickly roll tightly around a pencil. Transfer to a wire rack to cool, seam side down.

With a pastry bag or soda straw or wooden pick, fill rolls with Creamy Chocolate Filling.

To Make Filling: In a small saucepan, melt chocolate and 1/4 teaspoon of vegetable oil (or butter or margarine) over low heat stirring constantly.

Cereal Chocolate Roll Recipe

Ingredients

3/4 cup corn syrup
3/4 cup white sugar
2 tablespoons butter
4 1/2 cups crisp rice cereal
1/3 cup butter
3 tablespoons milk
1 1/2 cups confectioners' sugar
2/3 cup unsweetened cocoa powder
3/4 cup peanut butter

Directions

Melt together corn syrup and white sugar over low heat. When mixture bubbles, remove from heat and add peanut butter, butter or margarine, and crispy rice cereal.

Grease cookie sheet and put wax paper (also greased) on cookie sheet. Spread cereal mixture on wax paper.

To Make Filling: Mix together 1/3 cup butter or margarine, milk and confectioners' sugar. Stir in cocoa and mix well.

Spread filling on cereal mixture and roll up as for jelly roll. Slice when cool. Store in refrigerator.

Chocolate Orange Truffles

Ingredients

1/4 cup unsalted butter
3 tablespoons heavy cream
4 (1 ounce) squares semisweet chocolate, chopped
2 tablespoons orange liqueur
1 teaspoon grated orange zest
4 (1 ounce) squares semisweet chocolate, chopped
1 tablespoon vegetable oil

Directions

In a medium saucepan over medium-high heat, combine butter and cream. Bring to a boil, and remove from heat. Stir in 4 ounces chopped chocolate, orange liqueur, and orange zest; continue stirring until smooth. Pour truffle mixture into a shallow bowl or a 9X5 in loaf pan. Chill until firm, about 2 hours.

Line a baking sheet with waxed paper. Shape chilled truffle mixture by rounded teaspoons into small balls (a melon baller also works well for this part). Place on prepared baking sheet. Chill until firm, about 30 minutes.

In the top of a double boiler over lightly simmering water, melt remaining 4 ounces chocolate with the oil, stirring until smooth. Cool to lukewarm.

Drop truffles, one at a time, into melted chocolate mixture. Using 2 forks, lift truffles out of the chocolate, allowing any excess chocolate to drip back into the pan before transferring back onto baking sheet. Chill until set.

Recipe For Chocolate Chip Walnut Pie

Ingredients

3/4 cup packed light brown sugar
1/2 cup all-purpose flour
1/2 teaspoon baking powder
1/4 teaspoon ground cinnamon
2 eggs, lightly beaten
1 cup semi-sweet chocolate chips
1 cup coarsely chopped walnuts
1 (9 inch) pie shell, baked
1/2 cup heavy cream, chilled
1 tablespoon confectioners' sugar
1/4 teaspoon vanilla extract
1/4 teaspoon ground cinnamon
1 pinch ground nutmeg

Directions

Preheat oven to 350 degrees F (175 degrees C).

In a bowl, stir together brown sugar, flour, baking powder, and 1/4 teaspoon cinnamon. Add eggs, stir until blended. Stir in chocolate chips and walnuts. Pour into baked pie crust.

Bake at 350 degrees F (175 degrees C) for 25 to 30 minutes until lightly browned and set. Serve slightly warm or at room temperature with spiced cream.

To Make Spiced Cream: Mix together whipping cream, confectioners' sugar, vanilla, 1/4 teaspoon cinnamon, and nutmeg.

Chocolate Chocolate Chip Cookies III Recipe

Ingredients

1 1/2 cups all-purpose flour
1 1/2 teaspoons baking powder
1/4 teaspoon salt
2 cups semisweet chocolate chips
6 tablespoons butter, softened
1 cup white sugar
1 1/2 teaspoons vanilla extract
2 eggs
1/2 cup confectioners' sugar

Directions

Combine flour, baking powder and salt. Set aside.

Melt 1 cup of chocolate chips over low heat. Cream butter and sugar. Add melted chocolate chips and vanilla; beat in eggs; add flour mixture and remaining chocolate chips.

Wrap in plastic and freeze until firm (about 20 minutes).

Make small balls (1 inch); roll in confectioners' sugar. Place on ungreased cookie sheet and bake for 10-12 minutes at 350 degrees F (175 degrees C). Cool on wire rack.

Chocolate Decadence Cake III

Ingredients

16 (1 ounce) squares bittersweet chocolate
10 tablespoons butter
4 eggs
1 tablespoon white sugar
1 tablespoon all-purpose flour

Directions

Preheat oven to 400 degrees F (200 degrees C). Grease and flour an 8 inch round pan.

In the top of a double boiler, melt the chocolate and butter. Stir until smooth and remove from heat.

In a separate bowl over boiling water, whisk the eggs and sugar until light and lemon colored. Remove from heat and fold in the flour. Mix 1/4 of the egg mixture into the chocolate. Pour remaining egg mixture into chocolate and quickly fold until no streaks remain. Pour into prepared pan.

Bake at 400 degrees F (200 degrees C) for 15 minutes. The cake will be soft and appear under-baked. Allow to cool before removing from pan.

How To Make Ally's Chocolate Chip Cookies

Ingredients

3 cups rolled oats
1 cup milk
2 cups all-purpose flour
1 teaspoon baking soda
1 teaspoon salt
1 cup margarine
1 cup packed brown sugar
1/2 cup white sugar
2 eggs
1 teaspoon vanilla extract
1 cup semisweet chocolate chips

Directions

Preheat oven to 350 degrees F (175 degrees C). Soak the rolled oats in the milk for at least ten minutes.

Sift together the flour, baking soda and salt, set aside. In a medium bowl, cream together the margarine, brown sugar and white sugar. Stir in the eggs and vanilla. Add the sifted ingredients, and mix well. Then stir in the oat mixture and chocolate chips.

Drop dough by heaping spoonfuls onto the prepared cookie sheets. Bake for 12 to 15 minutes in the preheated oven, until cookies are golden brown. Cool on baking sheets or remove to cool on wire racks.

Chocolate Orange Fudge Recipe

Ingredients

2 1/2 cups semisweet chocolate chips
1 (14 ounce) can sweetened condensed milk
1/2 cup chopped pecans
2 teaspoons grated orange peel

Directions

Line an 8 x 8 inch square pan with parchment paper.

Melt chocolate chips with condensed milk in the top of a double boiler or in a bowl in the microwave. Stir until smooth. Remove from heat and stir in pecans and grated orange peel.

Pour chocolate mixture into prepared pan. Chill 2 hours, or until firm, and cut into squares. Store, covered, in the refrigerator.

Chocolate Hazelnut Teacake Recipe

Ingredients

1/2 cup butter
3 (1 ounce) squares bittersweet chocolate, chopped
2/3 cup white sugar
1 cup all-purpose flour
1/4 teaspoon baking soda
1/4 teaspoon baking powder
1/2 cup sour cream
2 eggs

1 teaspoon vanilla extract
1/2 cup ground roasted hazelnuts

Directions

Preheat oven to 325 degrees F (165 degrees C). Grease and flour an 8×4 inch loaf pan.

In a saucepan over medium heat, melt the butter, stir in the chocolate, remove from heat and stir until the chocolate is completely melted. Add the sugar and mix well. Combine the flour, baking powder and baking soda, stir into the chocolate mixture. Blend in the sour cream. Beat in the eggs one at a time, then stir in the vanilla. Finally, fold in the ground hazelnuts. Spread the batter evenly into the prepared pan.

Bake for 45 to 50 minutes in the preheated oven, or until a toothpick inserted into the cake comes out clean. Allow cake to cool for 10 minutes in the pan before inverting onto a wire rack to cool completely.

Chewy Chocolate Cookies III

Ingredients

2/3 cup shortening
1 1/2 cups packed brown sugar
1 tablespoon water
1 teaspoon vanilla extract
2 eggs
1 1/2 cups all-purpose flour
1/3 cup unsweetened cocoa powder
1/2 teaspoon salt
1/4 teaspoon baking soda
2 cups semisweet chocolate chips
1/2 cup chopped walnuts

Directions

In large bowl cream shortening, sugar, water and vanilla extract. Beat in eggs. In a separate bowl, combine flour, cocoa, salt and baking soda and gradually add to creamed mixture. Beat until just blended. Stir in chocolate chips and nuts.

Drop by rounded teaspoonfuls 2 inches apart on ungreased cookie sheets. Bake at 375 degrees F (190 degrees C) for 7 – 9 minutes. Do not overbake. Cool 2 minutes before removing from cookie sheet.

Recipe For Totally Groovy Chocolate Fondue

Ingredients

2 cups milk chocolate chips
3 tablespoons heavy cream
2 tablespoons cherry brandy
1 tablespoon strong brewed coffee
1/8 teaspoon ground cinnamon

Directions

Combine chocolate, cream, brandy, coffee and cinnamon in a fondue pot over a low flame (or in a saucepan over low heat). Heat until melted, stirring occasionally. Serve at once.

Chocolate Roll II

Ingredients

9 tablespoons all-purpose flour
6 tablespoons unsweetened cocoa powder
1 teaspoon baking powder
1/2 teaspoon salt6 egg yolks
4 egg whites
1 cup white sugar
1 teaspoon vanilla extract

1 cup packed brown sugar
2 tablespoons water
2 egg whites
1/4 cup confectioners' sugar for dusting

Directions

Preheat oven to 350 degrees F (175 degrees C). Line a 10×15 inch jelly roll pan with parchment paper. Stir together the flour, cocoa, baking powder, and salt; set aside.

In a large bowl, beat egg yolks until thick and pale yellow. Fold in flour mixture. In a large glass or metal mixing bowl, beat 4 egg whites until foamy. Gradually add white sugar, continuing to beat until stiff peaks form. beat in vanilla. Fold 1/3 of the whites into the batter, then quickly fold in remaining whites until no streaks remain. Pour batter into prepared pan.

Bake in preheated oven for 12 to 14 minutes, or until cake springs back when lightly tapped. Turn cake out onto a towel dusted with confectioners' sugar, and roll up until cool.

To Make Frosting: In a small saucepan, stir together brown sugar and water. Cook, stirring constantly, until sugar spins a thread when dropped from a spoon. In a large bowl, beat together remaining 2 egg whites until foamy. Slowly pour brown sugar liquid into egg whites while beating. Beat until frosting forms stiff peaks. Unroll cake and apply frosting in an even layer. Roll cake back up and refrigerate.

Recipe For Maple Hot Chocolate

Ingredients

1/4 cup sugar
1 tablespoon baking cocoa
1/8 teaspoon salt
1/4 cup hot water
1 tablespoon butter or margarine
4 cups milk
1 teaspoon maple flavoring

1 teaspoon vanilla extract
12 large marshmallows

Directions

In a large saucepan, combine sugar, cocoa and salt. Stir in hot water and butter; bring to a boil. Add the milk, maple flavoring, vanilla and 8 marshmallows. Heat through, stirring occasionally, until marshmallows are melted. Ladle into mugs and top each with a marshmallow.

How To Make White Chocolate Chunk Cookies

Ingredients

1/2 cup butter, softened
1/2 cup shortening
3/4 cup white sugar
1/2 cup packed brown sugar
1 egg
1 3/4 cups all-purpose flour
1 teaspoon baking soda
1/2 teaspoon salt
2 teaspoons vanilla extract
10 ounces white chocolate, chopped
1/2 cup chopped and toasted macadamia nuts

Directions

In a large bowl, cream butter and shortening; gradually add sugars, beating well at medium speed with an electric mixer. Beat in egg and vanilla. Combine flour, soda, and salt; stir into creamed mixture. Stir in white chocolate and macadamia nuts. Chill dough for 1 hour.

Preheat oven to 350 degrees F (175 degrees C). Lightly grease cookie sheets. Drop dough by heaping tablespoonfuls 3 inches apart onto prepared cookie sheets.

Bake for 12 to 14 minutes in preheated oven. Cookies will be soft. Cool slightly on cookie sheets; transfer to wire racks to cool completely.

Chocolate Raspberry Dessert

Ingredients

1 cup 1% cottage cheese
3/4 cup fat-free milk
1/3 cup raspberry spreadable fruit
1 (1.4 ounce) package sugar-free instant chocolate pudding mix
1 (8 ounce) container frozen reduced-fat frozen whipped topping, thawed
1 (1 ounce) square semisweet chocolate, melted
1/2 cup unsweetened raspberries

Directions

In a blender, combine cottage cheese, milk and spreadable fruit; cover and process until smooth. Add pudding mix and mix well. Pour into a bowl; fold in whipped topping. Spoon into a 9-in. pie plate. Drizzle with chocolate. Cover and freeze for 8 hours or overnight. Let stand at room temperature for 20 minutes before serving. Garnish with raspberries.

Original NestleB(r) Toll HouseB(r) Chocolate Chip Cookies

Ingredients

2 1/4 cups all-purpose flour
1 teaspoon baking soda
1 teaspoon salt
1 cup butter or margarine, softened
3/4 cup granulated sugar
3/4 cup packed brown sugar
1 teaspoon vanilla extract

2 large egg
1 (12 ounce) package NESTLEB(r) TOLL HOUSEB(r) Semi-Sweet Chocolate Morsels
1 cup chopped nuts

Directions

PREHEAT oven to 375 degrees F.

COMBINE flour, baking soda and salt in small bowl. Beat butter, granulated sugar, brown sugar and vanilla extract in large mixer bowl until creamy. Add eggs one at a time, beating well after each addition. Gradually beat in flour mixture. Stir in morsels and nuts. Drop by rounded tablespoon onto ungreased baking sheets.

BAKE for 9 to 11 minutes or until golden brown. Cool on baking sheets for 2 minutes; remove to wire racks to cool completely.

BAKER'S Classic Chocolate Fudge Recipe

Ingredients

2 (8 ounce) packages BAKER'S Semi-Sweet Baking Chocolate
1 (14 ounce) can sweetened condensed milk
2 teaspoons vanilla
1 cup chopped PLANTERS Walnuts

Directions

Line 8-inch square pan with foil, with ends of foil extending over sides of pan. Set aside. Microwave chocolate and milk in large microwaveable bowl on HIGH 2 to 3 min. or until chocolate is almost melted, stirring after 2 min. Stir until chocolate is completely melted. Blend in vanilla. Stir in walnuts.

Spread into prepared pan.

Refrigerate 2 hours or until firm. Lift fudge from pan, using foil handles. Cut into 48 pieces.

Victory Chocolate Cake

Ingredients

2 cups sifted all-purpose flour
2 1/4 teaspoons baking soda
3/4 cup shortening
1 1/2 cups dark corn syrup
1 1/2 teaspoons vanilla extract
1/2 cup unsweetened cocoa powder
3/4 teaspoon salt
1/3 cup white sugar
3 eggs
1 cup cold, brewed coffee

Directions

Preheat oven to 350 degrees F (175 degrees C). Grease one 9×13 inch pan.

Sift together the flour, cocoa, baking soda, and salt; set aside.

Separate eggs. Beat egg whites in a clean bowl until stiff peaks form.

Cream shortening and sugar in mixing bowl until light and fluffy using electric mixer at medium speed. Blend in the corn syrup and egg yolks. Beat in vanilla. Add dry ingredients alternately with coffee to creamed mixture. Gently fold in egg whites. Pour batter into greased 13×9 inch pan.

Bake in preheated 350 degree F (175 degree C) oven for 45 minutes or until cake is done. Cool in pan on rack and frost as desired.

How To Make Chocolate Pudding Cake III

Ingredients

3/4 cup all-purpose flour
2/3 cup white sugar

1/2 cup unsweetened cocoa powder
1 1/2 teaspoons baking powder
1/2 teaspoon salt
1/2 cup milk
3 tablespoons vegetable oil
2/3 cup packed brown sugar
1/4 cup miniature semisweet chocolate chips
1 teaspoon vanilla extract
1 1/4 cups hot water

Directions

Preheat oven to 350 degrees F (175 degrees C).

In an 8×8 inch square pan, stir together the flour, white sugar, 1/4 cup of cocoa, baking powder and salt. Add milk and oil, mix well. Sprinkle brown sugar, remaining cocoa and chocolate chips over the mixture. Add the vanilla to the hot water, then pour the water over the top.

Bake for 30 to 35 minutes in the preheated oven, until the surface appears dry. Serve warm with a spoon or at room temperature.

www.ingramcontent.com/pod-product-compliance
Lightning Source LLC
Chambersburg PA
CBHW081625100526
44590CB00021B/3612